My
Milk Shake

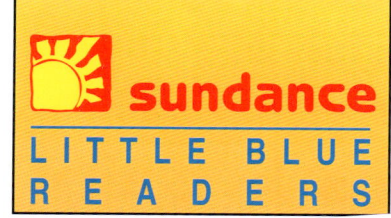

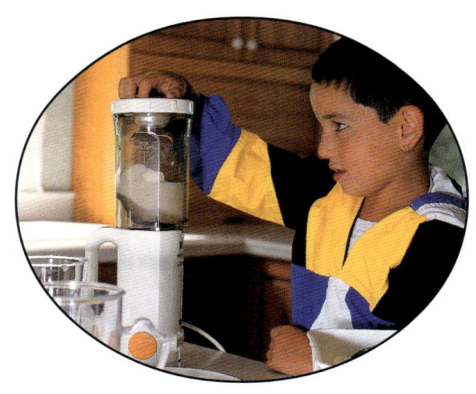

Focus: Systems

PETER SLOAN &
SHERYL SLOAN

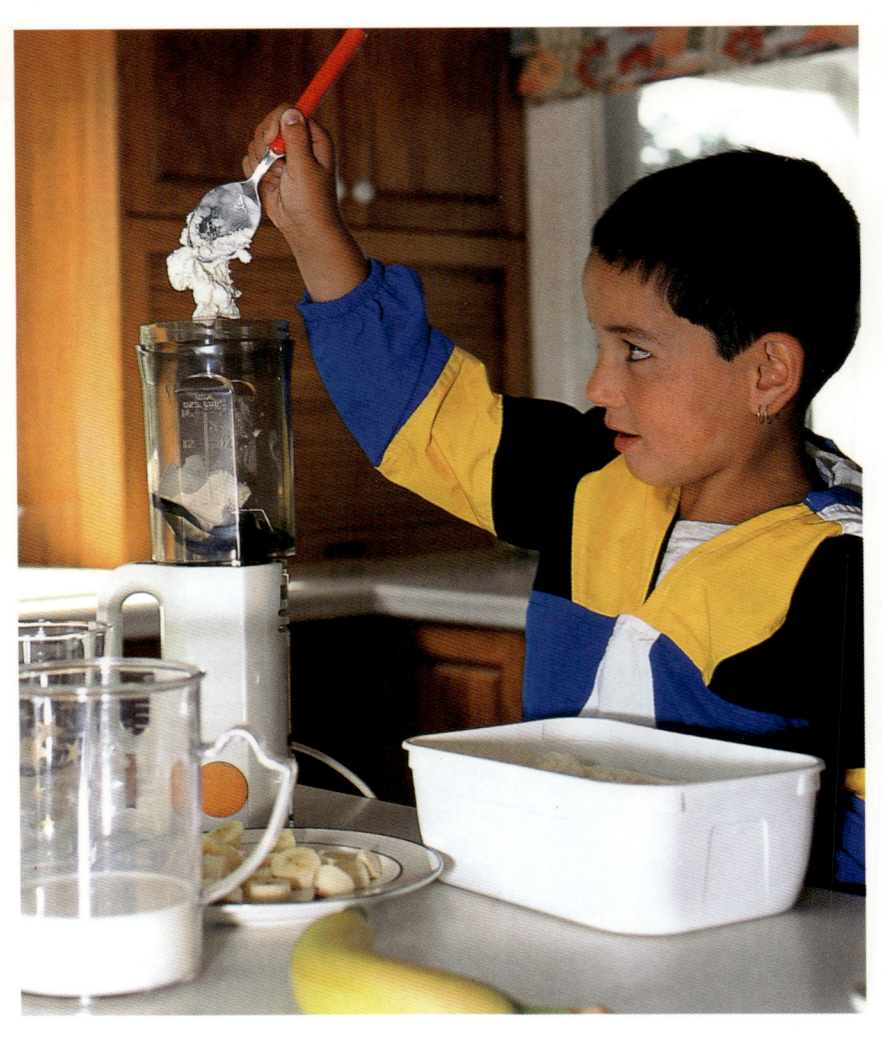

I put ice cream in the blender.

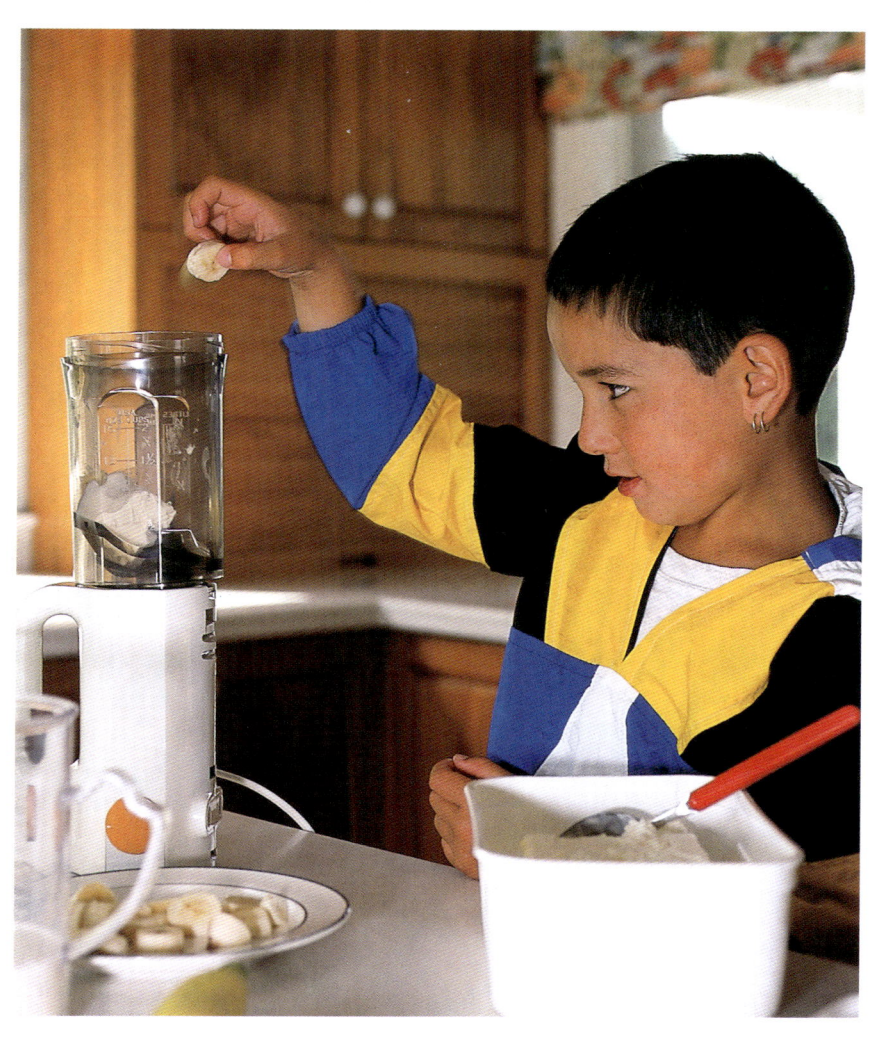

I put banana
in the blender.

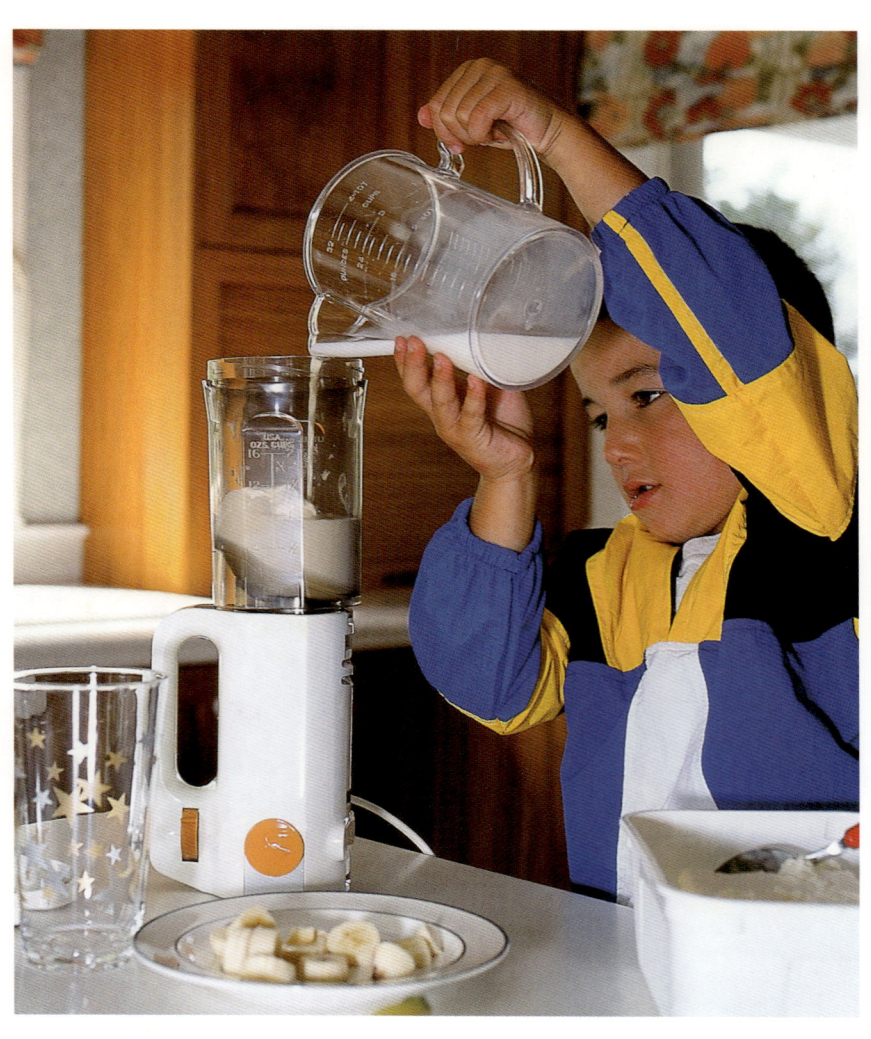

I put milk
in the blender.

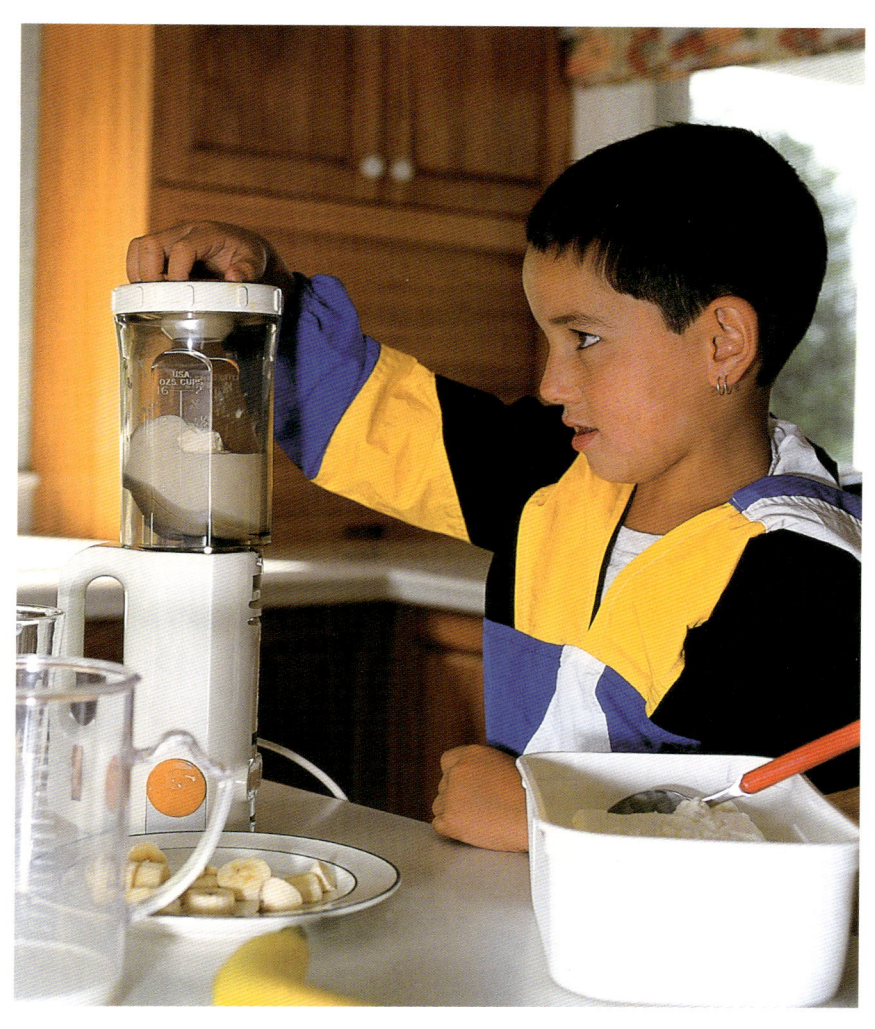

I put the lid
on the blender.

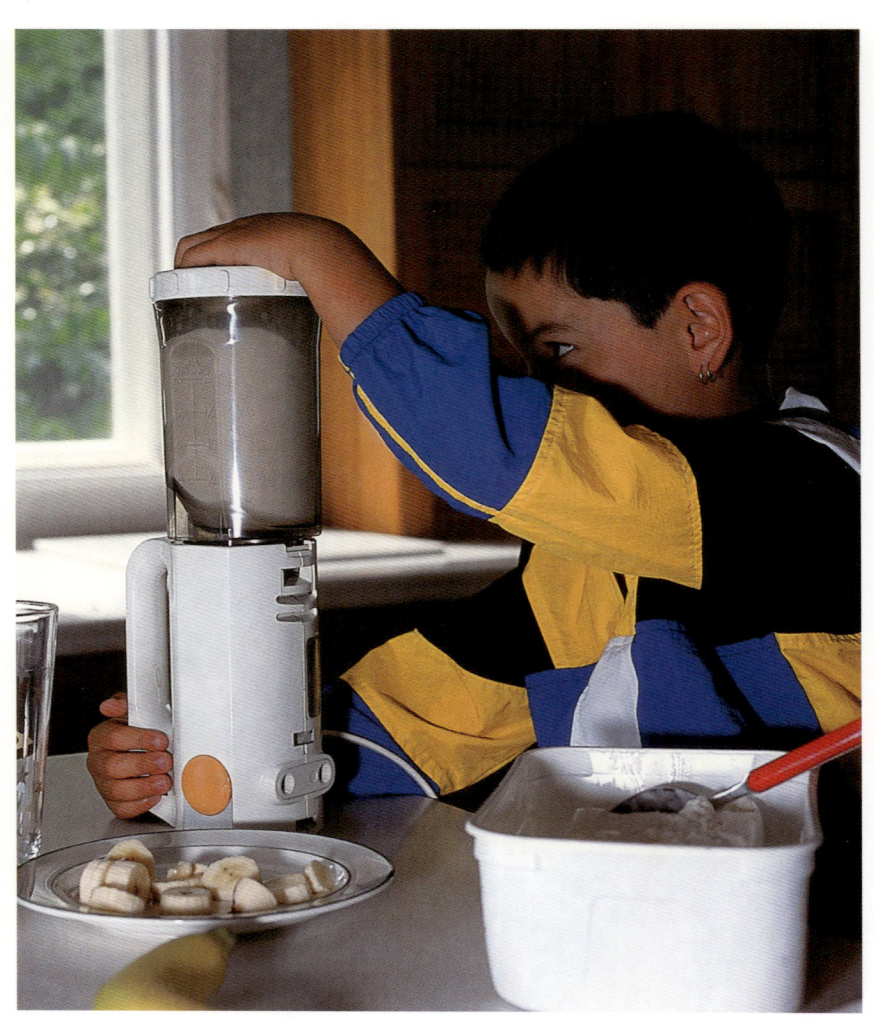

I switched on
the blender.

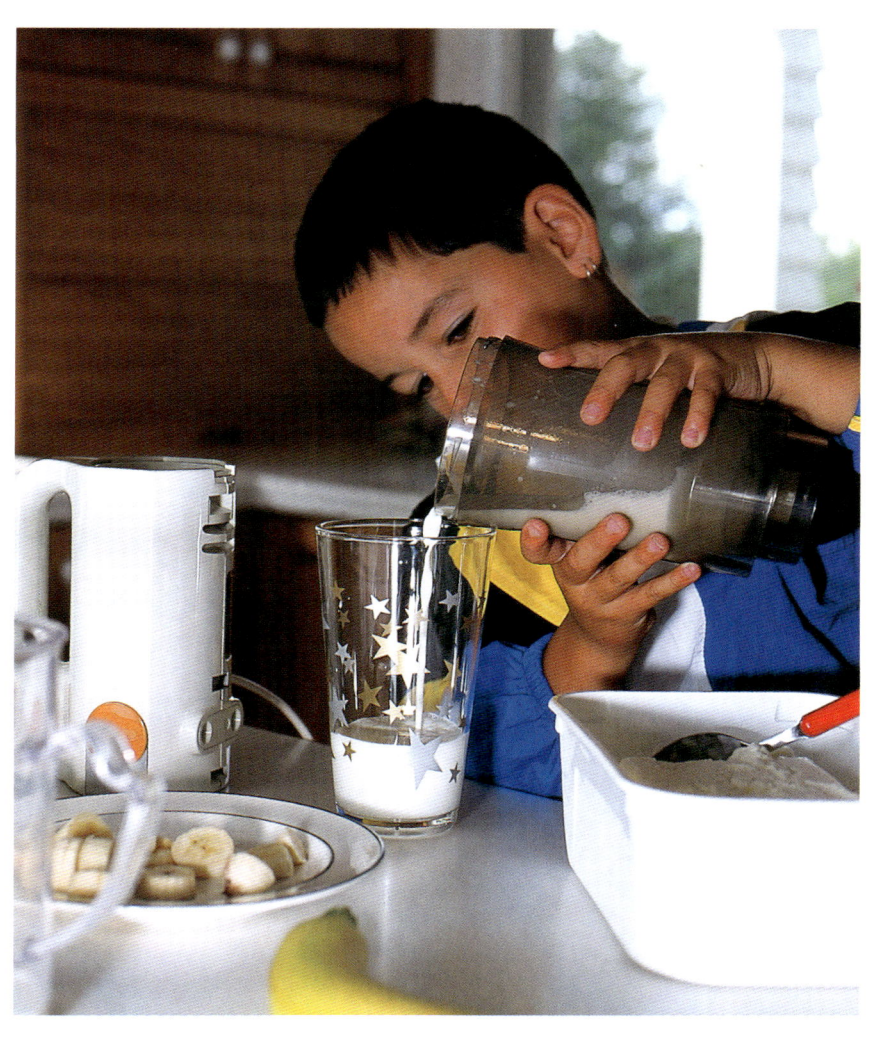

I poured
my milk shake.

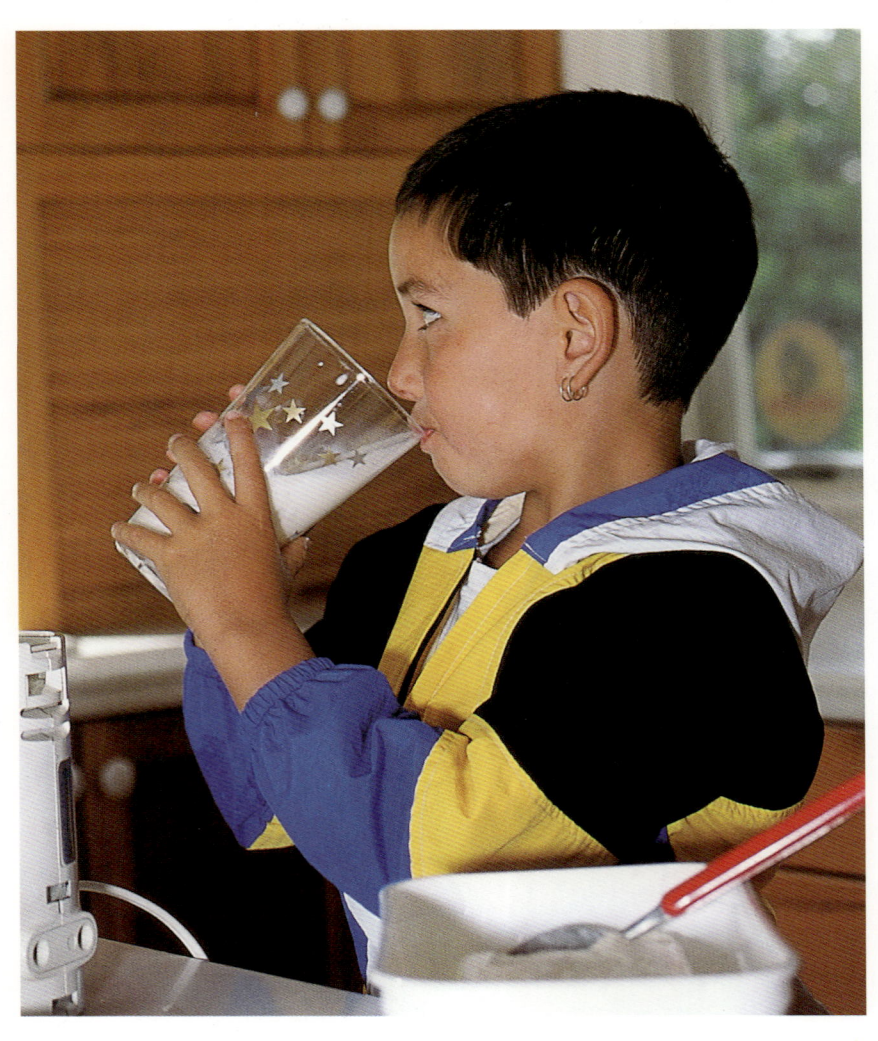

I drank
my milk shake.